Praise for
Relationship on Purpose

While there are many books about marriage in the marketplace, this book is unique. Barry has really created more of a handbook with practical strategies that you can put into practice immediately to improve your relationship. If you want to experience rapid positive change in your marriage, I recommend these 8 strategies.

Gary Chapman, Author of *The Five Love Languages*

Marriage can be a difficult and often treacherous road to navigate. Barry Ham is an excellent relationship guide to help route us through and around many of the obstacles, potholes, and detours along the pathways of life. These 8 simple yet powerful and practical principles will serve as a valuable compass and map to help steer us on a wonderful and adventurous marital journey!

Jared Pingleton, Psy.D., Clinical Psychologist and Minister Author of "*Making Magnificent Marriages*," and seven other books

D1706438

This new book from my friend Barry Ham is nothing less than a life preserver for your marriage or other relationships. The eight practical keys, if applied, can turn around any relationship and put it on the road to being healthy. I personally found several keys that I believe will thoroughly enhance my way of interacting with everyone I come in contact with.

Brad Herman
Publisher, Harrison House

Nearly every couple I have encountered has times where they feel distant, misunderstood, unseen, or unheard. Based on his 25 years of clinical experience, in *Relationship on Purpose,* Dr. Barry Ham shares powerful practical tips and strategies for every couple to find intimacy with God and each other.

Tim Clinton, Ed.D.
President, American Association of Christian Counselors
Co-Host, Family Talk Radio

Brimming over with professional and experiential examples, this is a practical volume that will help both the clinician as well as the lay person ameliorate communication mishaps in marriage. Predicated on God's plan for marriage, yet not religious, Barry Ham refreshingly nails it with a humanistic approach that is guaranteed to improve any relationship. *Relationship on Purpose* is a must-have for all who have said "I do" but find themselves in the conundrum of second-guessing that they ever did.

Nathaniel Granger, Jr., PsyD - Director, Be REAL Ministries; Past-President, Society for Humanistic Psychology (American Psychological Association, Division 32)

Even the most committed and loving marriages will face stress, conflict, and misunderstanding. Many devoted couples find their relationships suffering without knowing exactly how they got there. In *Relationship on Purpose*, Dr. Barry Ham offers eight specific strategies geared toward avoiding the most common pitfalls in marriage. If you'll take his advice to heart and implement the tools he lays out, you're sure to see your relationship with your spouse grow, deepen, and even flourish.

Dr. Greg Smalley, Vice President of Marriage at Focus on the Family

Relationship

On

Purpose

Relationship On Purpose

8 Strategies Guaranteed to Improve Your Marriage or Significant Relationship

BARRY D. HAM PH.D.

Thomas Quinn Nolan Books
A Publication of IFIT

Thomas Quinn Nolan Books
Colorado Springs, CO

ISBN: 9798537440581

Printed in the United States of America.

This book is dedicated to all of the courageous men and women who refuse to be satisfied with the status quo and are committed to building their relationship on, and with, purpose!

OTHER BOOKS BY BARRY HAM

Living on Purpose: Knowing God's Design For Your Life

Married on Purpose: A 91 Day Devotional to Ignite Your Most Intimate Relationship

Unstuck: Escaping the Rut of a Lifeless Marriage

God Understands Divorce: A Biblical Message of Grace

Contents

ACKNOWLEDGMENTS

With the completion of every book project, I am grateful and humbled by all of the assistance and support of those involved in bringing it to life.

I wish to first thank my wife Andee, whose eyeballs are always the first to see each chapter as they come off of the printer. She has a great eye for catching the smallest of errors that I miss. She also provides a fresh, and the first objective, perspective of the material. And on top of that, she lives *Relationship on Purpose* with me on a daily basis. Thank you.

My editor, Amy Calkins, is the best. She makes smoothing out the bumps and tightening up a manuscript look easy, which is a testament to her skills. I am also grateful to Renz my cover designer, who was more than patient and accommodating as we worked through various designs and numerous tweaks. Thanks for your graciousness and creativity.

I am blessed by my dear friends in our small group – Brent, Andrea, Larry, Lynn, Ed, and Noemi. Thanks for your input into the process.

To my friend and publishing advisor, Brad Herman of Harrison House Publishing, I always appreciate your wisdom and guidance in my various endeavors. You always go above and beyond. Thank you.

And finally – I am humbled by the fact that the God of the Universe would continue to use this broken vessel of a person in some small way to impact the trajectory of other people's lives. It is truly a privilege that I don't deserve but I cherish the opportunity. It is for Your glory that I write!

Chapter One – Introduction – In the Beginning . . .

"The great marriages are partnerships. It can't be a great marriage without being a partnership." – Helen Mirren

"Alone we can do so little; together we can do so much." – Helen Keller

It was a delightful sunny afternoon as David and Michelle stood before their family and friends, taking their sacred vows of marriage in the shadow of Colorado's Pike's Peak. This was a day that had been coming ever since they first met at a gathering of friends three years earlier. Their courtship had been careful and somewhat methodical, as they didn't want to make a mistake. They had both seen friends rush into unwise situations. One couple they knew had gotten married 28 days after meeting. Another moved in together after dating for a week. Both relationships had not lasted. They were determined not to make the same type of mistakes.

David believed he had hit the jackpot when he began dating Michelle. She was witty, she was fun to hang out with, and on top of that, she was beautiful. He was impressed with her unwavering faith, even though she had been through many health challenges as a kid. She was perfect.

Michelle and begun to think that all guys "were pigs," as she was heard to frequently say. They were only "interested in one thing," or they were only about themselves. But David—now he was different. He was respectful, steady, and dependable, a man of faith and integrity, and he treated her like she mattered.

So, here they were—having taken careful steps to build their relationship with a solid foundation and listened to the wisdom of their parents and the advice of trusted friends, they knew they were meant to be together and were destined for a beautiful and fulfilling life together. And they were . . . but perhaps with a few bumps along the way.

About This Book

We will pick up David and Michelle's story a bit later. But first I want to explain why I have written this book and just what you can expect to gain from it.

I became a Marriage and Family Therapist in 1995 and have been a university professor of Relationship and Marriage and Family courses since 1990. Over more than a quarter of a century (I sound ancient when I put it like that, but anyone who knows me knows I am really just this side of ancient), I have observed relatively consistent patterns of behavior in individuals and couples. At the same time, I have tried various approaches to help my clients and students gain the skills they need to grow happy, fulfilling relationships. Some tools have been somewhat helpful or worked with limited success. However, after 25 years of doing this work, I have arrived at eight strategies that consistently work to improve relationships. This book is about helping you develop the relationship you have always dreamed of having. And these eight strategies can empower and enable you to get there.

I want to communicate three significant things about this book. First, it is not intended to be a lengthy book with lots of theories and philosophical foundations. It is intended to be a practical book that empowers you with you can immediately begin to use. It does not require you to give great thought to these concepts before you can begin to implement them. Pondering is not a prerequisite.

They are skills that are ready to use (no batteries or assembly required). Think of this book as more of a practical handbook or reference guide.

Second, I want to address the title and sub-title of this book. The title, *Relationship on Purpose,* refers to the way in which the vast majority of couples seem to stumble into relationships and just sort of go along for the ride, whatever that turns out to be. But marriage was designed with and for purpose. God knew what He was doing when He created the concept of marriage. He made this partnership first and foremost so that we wouldn't be alone, so that we would have a companion to help us in the journey and to share and enjoy life with (Gen. 2:18). That helping, sharing, and enjoying doesn't just magically happen. It requires purposeful intentionality. The subtitle is: *8 Strategies Guaranteed to Improve Your Marriage or Significant Relationship.* Allow me to deconstruct this a little bit. First, lots of marriage tools exist—many more than eight. But these eight are the ones I have discovered are essential to healthy marriages in my 25 years of working with couples. Next is the word *guaranteed.* Now, you might be thinking, "You must have a screw loose. How can you guarantee to fix my marriage. It is a train wreck. Nobody can make this wonderful." And I would agree with you (well, maybe not the screw loose part, though others might). I can't fix your marriage or relationship. But I can guarantee that these eight strategies will improve your marriage *if*.... "If? If what? See, I knew there was a catch." Nope, there is no catch. I can guarantee that this skills will improve your relationship if – you use them.

In my counseling practice, I have found that those couples who are intentional about learning and using the tools begin to make progress and start enjoying their relationship again rather quickly, while those who give lip service to the skills but don't use them simply spin their wheels. However, if you diligently embrace, learn, practice, and use them, I promise your marriage will improve.

I often use this ridiculous example with clients and students. I remember, back in the days before nail guns were prevalent, that I was frequently amazed at the great skill of accomplished carpenters. They were able to take a large nail and, with about two swings of their hammer, drive that nail into a 4X4 post. Yet, when I attempted to do it, I found myself going "whack, whack, whack, whack, whack" (on and on) before I achieved the same result. But this is understandable. They were skilled craftsmen; me, not so much.

Now imagine (this is where is gets absurd) that I invite my carpenter friend to come over to my house on the weekend to help me change the spark plugs in my car. He graciously agrees and arrives at my house on Saturday to help me. I open the hood of my car and say, "There it is. We need to get the old plugs out first."

He says, "OK," and pulls out his hammer and begins to wail on the engine. He is hammering away with the same force as when he drives nails into a post, denting engine parts as he goes.

I holler, "Whoa! Stop! What are you doing?"

He responds, "I'm going to get your spark plugs out."

I adamantly assert, "No you're not! You may break them off, but you will not get them out!"

So, he asks, "Well, then how do I do it?"

I begin to show him how to use a socket wrench to remove them. "The socket goes over the spark plug, and you use the wrench forearm motion to turn the socket, which then unscrews the spark plug."

He takes the wrench and begins to try it. It is a very different motion from what he is used to, as he normally swings with the power of his entire arm in a forward motion. My friend says, "Hmm, that's different." Then he sets down the wrench, pulls out his hammer, and begins to beat up the engine again.

With stunned disbelief, I stop him and say, "Why are you doing that? It doesn't work!"

He simply responds, "Because I'm good at it!"

We are often times like that carpenter. We snap at our spouse; we put them down; we attempt to bully them to get them to do what we want; we embarrass them in front of friends; we insult them; we selfishly ignore their needs; and the list goes on. Do these approaches improve our relationship with them? Absolutely not! Then why do we continue with those behaviors? Because we are good at them. And we are so good at them that we don't even have to think about them. We can simply be on auto-pilot and be unkind and unloving with the best of them. Most don't think of the consequences of their behavior; they just react without thinking and default to what they do so well. Again, it is not that those behaviors are effective; it is that they are easy, and we are good at them.

If you are ready to change your behaviors from what you are good at to behaviors that are guaranteed to improve your relationship, then you have come to the right place.

Third, I want to address the underlying values behind this book. While I have a strong belief in God and am a Jesus follower, that is in no way a requirement for you to benefit from this book. The practical nature of this book makes it useable for believers and non-believers alike. But I want you to know that it does come from God's value system, which infuses the strategies with divine purpose and imbues them with God's help. So even if you don't have a relationship with God, these strategies are based on godly principles and will still work for you. As a matter of fact, as the subtitle reflects, these strategies, when used, will not only improve your marriage, but they will also work with the person you're dating, a co-worker, your kids, and even your parents. In other words, these principles can be effectively implemented in any significant relationship. For most of us, our spouse is the most significant person we relate to and is the person with whom we may have the greatest difficulty maintaining healthy interactions. If we can learn to use these skills in our marriage, using them with other individuals becomes much easier.

Design

The pages that follow have two sections. The first section contains what I would refer to as the four basic tools, while the second section discusses the four advanced tools. As I have mentioned, these are practical, doable strategies. We will follow the journey of David and Michelle as they encounter the need to adopt and implement these skills; we will examine a step-by-step process of how to use each one; and we will observe examples of these tools in action.

If you are ready to embark on a journey that can change and reenergize your marriage and your most significant relationships – let's get started!

Questions to Contemplate

1. What relationship issue in your life most contributed to your decision to pick up this book?

2. What do you most hope to gain from this book?

3. Does the *if factor* (the strategies will work *if you use them*) make you nervous? If so, why might that be?

SECTION ONE

BASIC TOOLS

Chapter Two – "You Said What?"

"There's a lot of difference between listening and hearing." – G. K. Chesterton

"To learn through listening, practice it naively and actively. Naively means that you listen openly, ready to learn something, as opposed to listening defensively, ready to rebut. Listening actively means you acknowledge what you heard and act accordingly." – Betty Sanders

David was wandering through the tool section of Home Depot when his phone rang. He saw that it was Michelle so he quickly answered, "Hi Honey, what's up?"

With irritation in her voice, she responded, "Where are you?"

While he was caught off guard by her question, he simply and calmly said, "I'm at Home Depot."

"What? What are you doing there?"

David was confused by the question. He had clearly told her he was going to be out shopping and was going to stop to look at some tools. So, trying not to sound overly exasperated, he said, "Remember, I told you I was going to stop here to look at new drills?"

Michelle was quick to reply, "You didn't tell me that at all. You said you were going to run some errands and you would be back in an hour to help me move that dresser. Shelly will be here any minute to help me stain it, but it is not moved into the garage yet."

Now David was totally thrown by this statement. He was certain he had said he was going to look at tools and would be back in a little while. However, she had heard something completely different. How could this be?

Welcome to the World of Miscommunication

So what happened with David and Michelle? Was Michelle not paying attention to what David had told her? Or was David not clear in what he had said? Who knows? It could have been the mistake of one or the other, or neither, or both.

You see, when we communicate our thoughts, our words go through the prism of our own perspective. While we know what we are thinking and what we mean, we don't always communicate those thoughts accurately—even though we are convinced we do.

Similarly, when we hear what someone tells us, we hear it through the lens of our own world, interpreting what they say through our own expectations. We have been known to say, "I know what I heard." But whether or not that is accurate is up for discussion. Sometimes I think it is amazing that we are able to effectively communicate at all—given the differences of our viewpoints.

What makes it even more convoluted is that we make decisions and take actions based upon what we are convinced we said or are certain we heard. For example, based upon what Michelle "knew" David said, she had made plans for her friend Shelly to come over at a given time to help her stain the dresser. Needless to say, the two of them were not on the same page.

How many times have you found yourself in this situation, either absolutely knowing what you said or thoroughly convinced of what you heard? If you are like most couples, the answer is many! And based upon those assumptions, we have taken actions that have resulted in misunderstandings, at best, or feelings of being discounted and not important enough to be listened to, at worst. But this disconnect is avoidable.

Here is another example. A few years ago, I had a client call in a panic. He and his wife needed to get in to see me as soon as possible before his wife divorced him. He loved her and did not want to lose his marriage. As they sat in my office, something seemed off. He talked with a sense of urgency, while she seemed unruffled but appropriately engaged. The more calm she was, the more panicked he seemed.

Finally, he said to her, "Don't you even care? Doesn't our marriage mean anything to you?"

She responded, "Of course it does. Why are you so agitated?"

"Why am I so agitated? How can I not be when you are about to divorce me?"

Quite puzzled by his response, she replied, "What are you talking about? I never said I was going to divorce you!"

"You absolutely did! Last Friday you told me that you 'were done.' Why do you think I called Dr. Ham?"

Her response began to bring some clarity to the picture. "We had been arguing about the same issue for over an hour. I was tired of talking about it, so I told you that I was done."

They both knew what "I'm done" meant. Or at least they thought they did. But in actuality, they weren't even close. To him, "I'm done" indicated that she was done with the marriage and was going to pursue divorce. While to her, "I'm done" meant she was done with that particular conversation. They used the same two words, "I'm done." You wouldn't think it would be that difficult to understand. But, as you can see, their individual understanding of what was intended by those two words quickly became a mangled mess.

We have all been there! We can understand how the confusion can occur. "But what can we do to avoid it?"

I'm glad you asked. I want to introduce you to our first communication tool—**Reflective Listening.**

Reflective Listening

This skill is all about making sure we know not only what words the other person spoke, but what they meant by the words they used.

About 10 years ago, a couple I had been seeing came into my office one evening. As we were chit-chatting as they walked in, I nonchalantly inquired, "How has the week been?"

He responded, "It's been a great week!"

At which point, she said, "He's grounded."

With that statement, his head quickly turned toward her with a look of hurt and disbelief. I turned to her with equal surprise, wondering what had transpired this week that they saw so differently. But here is the kicker—they hadn't seen the week differently. She thought it had been a great week as well. You see, he and I both thought that we "knew" what she meant when she said, "He's grounded." We both believed she was indicating that he was in trouble for something and that he was now grounded, whatever that meant. But what she was saying was that it had been a great week because he is so grounded—even, steady, anchored, steadfast, dependable, etc. He was grounded.

The earlier couple had gotten tripped up on two words, "I'm done." This couple managed to get equally confused with just two words, "He's grounded."

Now fortunately, they were in my office, and I was able to ask a couple of questions, and   we quickly cleared up the confusion. At that point, this couple had not yet learned Reflective Listening. So, had they not been in my office, but at home, it is easy to imagine the conversa-

14

tion going something like this.

"I think we have had a pretty great week, don't you?"

"Well, you're grounded."

"What? What do you mean I'm grounded? I can't believe you just said that. There is just no pleasing you. I have done my best this week, but no matter what I do, it's never good enough. I'm still somehow in trouble with you. So, I have had it. I'm going over to Frank's to hang out. At least I won't be in trouble with him. So, don't call me. Just leave me alone."

When they finally talk the next day, if they do, they will realize the misunderstanding that took place and how avoidable it was.

Reflective Listening is a process of reflecting back to the person speaking what you heard them say. It is not a word-for-word repetition or a parroting of what the other person said. It is instead a reflection of concepts.

For example, with this couple that we just discussed, when she said, "He's grounded," he could have responded with something like, "When you say that I'm grounded, it sounds as though I'm in some kind of trouble. Am I understanding you correctly?"

"Oh no, not at all. It really has been a great week, in part because you are so grounded and steadfast."

"Well, thanks. I was misunderstanding you for a minute there. But your explanation was nice to hear."

Or we could use the example with David and Michelle in a pre-emptive manner. While we don't know exactly what was said, we can approximate it as follows.

"Michelle I'm going to take off now to run some errands. I may stop and take a look at some tools as well."

"So, I know you said you are going to run some errands. Are you still planning to be back in an hour?"

"Not necessarily. I didn't say when I would be back. But

it sounds as though you are thinking I will be back sooner rather than later."

"Well, you did tell me yesterday that you would help me move the dresser to the garage before Shelly gets here at 11:00. Is that still your game plan?"

"Oh, so you thought I would be back in time to help you with that. I had forgotten all about it, so I'm glad you reminded me. Thanks. Yes, I will be sure to be back by then."

Reflective Listening checks in with the other person for understanding rather than assuming we know what they mean. As we have seen from a few examples, we can easily make an assumption that is unknowingly incorrect, which sets us up for a potential, but avoidable, conflict. And avoiding conflict is a step toward healthier and more enjoyable relationships.

When using Reflective Listening, a number of phrases can be easily used to begin the reflection, such as: "It sounds as though you are saying . . ."; "What I think I just heard you say was . . ."; "I want to make sure that I understood you to say . . ."; and other similar phrases.

Not Just Words

While we need to reflect what we have heard our mate say (or what we think they said), it is not only our words that communicate our thoughts. Facial expressions and other nonverbal cues are equally important and also indicate intent.

A number of years ago, a young couple in my office shared with me the following interaction. What I am about to describe was all nonverbal; the following conversation was only the thoughts taking place inside each person's head. Michael was in the entryway when his wife Wendy arrived home from work. As she walked in, she noticed that Michael had one eyebrow raised. She thought to herself, "I wonder what is wrong with him? The last time he had that kind of look on his face, he was upset with me about something, and it turned into a lecture. I am exhausted from work, and I don't have the energy to deal with his pettiness. I guess he will just have to be upset about whatever it is, but I'm not going to get into it with him." And with that, and without even uttering so much as a "Hi," she went into the other room.

As Wendy walked in, paused, and then walked right past Michael without saying anything, the conversation in his head went something like this. "What was that all about? She doesn't say, 'How are you,' 'Go jump in a lake,' or anything. I don't know if she had a bad day at work, but I don't deserve to be treated this way. I am in no mood for an argument, so I will leave her alone." And with that, he went into a different room.

As a result of these two separate internal conversations, of which neither was aware, they didn't talk to each other for two days. When they finally did speak, he discovered what Wendy had been thinking, and she learned that Michael was not upset with her and was unaware of any particular look on his face. They had unnecessarily been in silent treatment mode. What a wasted two days.

So, how could they have used Reflective Listening to avoid these icy positions? It is important to note that the responsibility for intervening with a reflective statement lies with both individuals. At any point in time, they both had the opportunity to use this strategy.

For example, when Wendy first came in the door and saw the look on Michael's face, she might have said, "Is everything OK? From the expression on your face, it seems as though you are upset about something."

With that one statement, she was likely to get a reply along the lines of, "No, I'm not upset with you at all. I'm not sure what look is on my face, but everything is fine. I'm just glad you are home." And with those respective statements, two days of missed interaction are avoided.

But what if Wendy fails to take advantage of the opportunity to use Reflective Listening? If she walks off to the other room without saying anything, Michael still has an opportunity to initiate a dialog using this skill. He could have perhaps said, "Honey, I couldn't help but notice when you came in that you avoided talking to me. It seems as though you may be upset with me about something. Is there anything I have done?"

She would likely reply, "No, I'm not upset. I just saw the expression on your face when I walked in, and you looked irritated. I didn't have the energy to engage in an argument. So I decided to go into another room and avoid the fight. It just seemed that you were upset. Did I misread your expression?"

"I guess so, because nothing is bothering me."

Again, two days of silence could be avoided by one person initiating a reflection of what they heard (or in this case saw), rather than making a false assumption leading to an inappropriate response leading to the train coming off the rails.

Reflective Listening is used for the purpose of understanding. By taking the time to clarify what we think we heard, we are much more likely to end up on the same page. In doing so, we eliminate false assumptions and reduce the risk of taking actions that are counter-productive.

Remember, as you try out this strategy, you will feel like the carpenter trying to use a socket wrench. It will be uncomfortable. It is far easier to just make mistaken assumptions and take actions that lead to conflict. But as you well know, taking the route that you don't have to think about is much more likely to lead to misunderstanding, harsh words, and hurt feelings.

Reflective Listening is a powerful and positive tool. If you will practice this strategy, using it often, it will eventually begin to feel comfortable and can become second nature. If you will use it consistently, I promise it will improve your relationship.

Question to Contemplate

1. Can you think of a situation when you have taken action based on what you thought you heard that turned out to be in error?

2. How frequently has conflict resulted from simply misunderstanding what your spouse intended to communicate?

3. What do you see as the biggest hurdle to employing the strategy of reflective listening?

Chapter Three – "You Make Me So Mad!"

As David pulled up to the house, having just driven home from a long day at work, he was greeted, once again, with the garage door standing wide open. It seemed lately that the garage was left open more than usual. David had called it to Michelle's attention, but it was beginning to seem as though the more he mentioned it, the worse the problem was becoming. Was this some passive-aggressive ploy on her part? Was she just trying to make him mad or what? He walked into the house loaded for bear.

"Hi Honey," Michelle greeted him.

Rather than respond in kind, David lit into her with, "I don't know if it is your goal to make me mad or what. But once again, the garage door is open, even after I have repeatedly asked you to make sure it is closed. You make me so mad when you ignore my requests!"

Stuck in Emotional Dishonesty

While it is understandable that David is upset that a repeated request seems to be ignored, did Michelle really make him mad? "Well," you might say, "It kind of seems so."

We have all, at one time or another, either said or had said to us the phrase, "You make me so mad." But is it really true? There is no question that we are angry, but did

21

the other person make us so? I would submit to you that when we make that statement, we are being emotionally dishonest.

We are a funny bunch of people. We don't want people messing with our stuff. "Don't touch my golf clubs," or, "I put that there for a reason, so please don't move it," or, "That's mine. Leave it alone." However, when it comes to what we perceive as our negative emotional stuff, we want to be as far away from that as possible. As a matter of fact, we are more than happy to let the other person mess with it. Actually, it is our preference that they do. We would much prefer to take it off of our plate and put it on theirs. You see, if we can make our negative emotions the other person's responsibility, "You make me so mad," then we are off the hook and don't have to deal with them. It is almost like we are innocently implying, "Well, I would be happy to own my part in this, but I didn't do anything. I was just minding my own business, being my calm sweet self, when they walked by and made me mad. I didn't want it to happen, but they did it to me, and there was nothing I could do to prevent it." But, I ask you, is that really true? I would submit that this is emotionally fraudulent.

While I would like to have power and influence, I don't have the power to make you mad. "What?" Yes, let me say it again. "I don't have the power to make you mad." Oh, I might be able to set the stage so that you are able to get angry a little easier, but you are still the only one who has power over your emotions. Let me give you an example.

Let's say you and your spouse walk into my office. You have on a blue shirt, and your mate has on a purple shirt. I casually mention that I had just read a research study that morning that stated that individuals who wore purple were typically found to be 20 percent smarter than people who wore other colors. Now if your husband or wife believed this, they might smile and say, "Well, that makes sense. I feel pretty good about hearing that."

But your facial expression might get knotted up and you might say, "I'm not less smart than they are. You make me so mad when you say that."

Wow! I must somehow have amazing powers. How did I do that? I said the same thing to both of you, but one of you is happy while the other is mad. How did I pull it off? The truth of the matter is that I didn't. I don't have that much power.

A significant underlying truth is: We feel what we feel because of what we believe. You see, if you and your spouse believe that what I was saying was factual, then the statement that people who wore purple were smarter would contribute to your partner feeling good about themselves. Likewise, if you believed that statement was true, it would be easy to understand why you might get upset. But here is the reality: You got upset; I didn't make you upset. The sooner we are able to see that, the sooner we are moving toward emotional honesty. Remember your mate's response when I made the statement to the two of you? They said, "I feel pretty good about hearing that." You see, when the feeling was positive, it was easy for them to embrace it and own the feeling—"I feel pretty good." But when the feeling is one we perceive as negative, we typically want to distance ourselves as much from it as we can. So we make a statement that makes those feelings someone else's responsibility—"You make me so mad."

If we believe being mad is a negative, then we don't want to own it. Likewise, if we believe feeling good is a positive, then we are happy to embrace it. As I said above, we feel what we feel because of what we believe about it. If we try to change our feelings, we are likely to have limited success. If I want to change my feelings, I will have much greater success if I tackle what I believe, making sure that my beliefs about the issue are accurate. That topic is a discussion for another time. I simply point out this truth so that you can be aware of the impact of your belief system on your emotions.

Moving Toward Emotional Honesty

When we blame our mate for our feelings, we create distance and walls between us and them. So, how do we avoid our propensity to do that? This second strategy that is guaranteed to improve our relationships is called an **I Message**. This strategy begins with a foundation of emotional honesty. It starts with identifying and owning our own feelings without blaming the other person.

An I Message contains three parts: 1) a statement of feeling 2) tied to a behavior by the other person 3) followed by a request for action. The basic formula looks like this: "I feel _____ (an emotion), when you do _____(a behavior or action), and I would like for you to do _____ (more of it, less of it, or something different).

Using the beginning scenario with David and Michelle, here is a specific example of how David could have used an I Message in his situation, as opposed to using a You Message that dishonestly blamed Michelle for his feelings. David would have done a much more effective job of building healthy connections had he used an I Message by saying, "I feel <u>angry</u> (an emotion) when <u>you leave the garage door open after I have asked you to be sure to close it when you get home</u> (a behavior or action), and I would like for you to <u>try to be more diligent about closing it</u> (a request to do something different)."

We need to remember that feelings are neither good nor

bad; they just are. The problems with feelings develop in how we handle them. If David says, "I feel angry when you leave the garage door open," that is a clear and respectful statement. There is nothing wrong with that, and there is nothing wrong with being angry. But if David had said, "I get so angry (no problem so far), when you are such an idiot, seemingly unable to do anything right, such as remembering to close the garage door." Now, damage has been done to Michelle. And while David started out with the makings of an I Message, it quickly deteriorated into a You Message and name calling.

An effective I Message communicates feelings while being respectful in its request. And here is the cool thing: I Messages are not only for negative situations; they can also be used for positive ones. For example, "I feel loved (an emotion) when you bring me flowers (an action), and I hope you will do that in the future (a request)." "I feel valued (an emotion) when you prepare a great dinner (an action), and I hope you will continue to do that (a request)."

There are two challenges to an I Message. The first one is in identifying emotions. You might think that this would be easy, but people really struggle to do this. I can, for example, ask a client what they are feeling and will often get a response like, "I think they shouldn't have done . . . ." I then have to remind them—that is a thought, not a feeling. Getting in touch with our feelings is important and necessary, but this leads us to the second challenge. One of the reasons we struggle with this is because discussing our feelings can leave us vulnerable. It gives the other person the opportunity to use our emotions to hurt us, if they so choose. For example. I might say, "I feel discounted when you don't listen when I am telling you something important." If you want to hurt me, you might respond with something like, "Good! I'm glad you feel discounted, because what you say doesn't really matter to me." Ugh—dagger in the heart. In situations like these, it's easy to think, "I should have stuck with what I thought instead of sharing what I felt." While I certainly understand those sentiments, we continue to try to identify our feelings because communicating our emotions with one another really lays the groundwork for genuine understanding and provides the opportunity for intimate bridge-building. While communicating thoughts can be nice, communicating our feelings can result in stronger heart connections.

Putting It into Practice

As you attempt to use the I Message formula, which sounds relatively simple, you will probably feel like the carpenter with the wrench. And when it becomes uncomfortable, it is easy to stop using the skill.

It is not uncommon, after I have taught a couple the I Message strategy and given them an assignment to practice it, for them to return having made little effort in this direction. I am always a little perplexed. But it is like using a socket wrench for them; it is a new tool, and it just doesn't feel quite right. You Messages are so much easier, and the individuals are so good at them (never mind that they only continue to harm the relationship) that they default to those dysfunctional patterns time and time again. When I inquire as to whether or not they have practiced their I Messages, I will frequently hear, "Maybe once or twice. We really didn't have much opportunity to use them." Allow me to translate that statement: "No, we didn't use them. They were uncomfortable and intimidating and felt emotionally risky. We avoided them like the plague."

So, we revisit the formula and practice a scenario from their week, in the office. One of them may begin with, "When she left the garage door open again, it made me feel angry." While he didn't blame her for his feelings, which is an improvement, he also didn't take ownership of them either. He said, "It made me feel . . . ." I am not sure who or what *it* is supposed to be, but *it* didn't make him feel anything. He got angry all by himself, and it is important that he learn to embrace the feeling.

If this couple experienced feelings this past week (which I am confident they did in an abundance), then they had opportunity to practice I Messages. As awkward as they may initially feel, couples who use this tool consistently will find, over time, that this strategy can become second nature and, surprisingly, will eventually become their default mode.

You can be that couple. You can practice this strategy until it becomes second nature. Using I Messages is guaranteed to improve your relationship!

Questions to Contemplate

1. Can you think of a situation when you have been emotionally dishonest?

2. What are your thoughts about the statement, "We feel what we feel because of what we believe"?

3. What will be your biggest challenge in effectively using the I Message strategy?

27

Chapter Four – "Listen to Me"

"Most people do not listen with the intent to understand; they listen with the intent to reply." – Stephen R. Covey

"IF we are to live together in peace, we must come to know each other better." – Lyndon Johnson

As Thanksgiving neared, Michelle was busy making plans. This would be the first time that she and David would be hosting The Feast, as her family liked to call it. Both sets of parents would be there, and this would be Michelle's very first time to tackle cooking a turkey. She was a little nervous and feeling the pressure to produce the most juicy, perfectly browned bird. The more she thought about it though, the more anxious she became.

It was ten days until the traditional holiday when David made a flippant remark one evening about how he hoped her first turkey wouldn't turn out to be too overcooked and dry. Unknowingly, David had just turned on the faucet of Michelle's tears. He sat bewildered, clueless as to exactly why Michelle was crying. Through her sobs, he could make out something about her fears around disappointing him as well as their parents. She tried to express how important it was to her to be the best hostess. David had not meant to upset her and attempted to express as much. But Michelle's rapid words continued to flow as she tried to reflect on what a great cook his mom was and how she was afraid that she couldn't measure up.

David said, "It wasn't my intent to imply that you wouldn't do a good job."

She responded, "If I don't make a great turkey, our parents will never want to have Thanksgiving at our home again."

"If I had known you were going to cry," David continued, "I wouldn't have said anything."

Michelle looked perplexed. She thought to herself, "David is not understanding what I am trying to say." So, she stated, "David, you don't understand."

"No," he shot back, "You don't understand!"

Trying to use her newly learned I Message skill, Michelle said, "I feel discounted when you keep talking about your perspective. I would really like for you to listen to what I am saying."

"Michelle, if you would just listen to what I'm trying to tell you, we could clear up this whole thing."

They seemed to be deadlocked, neither one really understanding the other.

We Can Work It Out
Try to see it my way,
Do I have to keep on talking till I can't go on?
While you see it your way
Run the risk of knowing that our love may soon be gone.

These Lennon and McCartney lyrics, from the song, "We Can Work it Out," accurately express what we often feel. It's easy to get into a conversation like David and Michelle were in. We are trying to get our point across to the other person, but we just don't feel as though they understand. So, rather than try to discover where the disconnect is, we just bear down more intensely, trying to get them to understand us. It reminds me of how my wife, who is an educator, would tell me the way teachers would frequently talk with Special Education students who did not understand a concept being taught. The teacher would attempt to get the student to understand by talking slower and louder. That didn't help. It just frustrated both the student and the teacher even more.

In their song, Lennon and McCartney basically seem to be saying, "If you will see things my way, then I won't have to keep on talking. But if you are determined that we see things your way, it could be the end of us." Hmm—that sounds pretty egotistical on the first person's part. They seem to think they have the correct perspective, and if everyone would just listen to them, then everything will be OK. But what they seem to be forgetting is that their viewpoint is not the only one. Someone else might have an equally valid perspective.

Yet, if we are honest, how many times have we felt like David or the person in the lyrics? We believe we have clear vision and a correct understanding of the situation. If our mate, child, friend, or coworker would just listen to us, then we would all be on the same page with the same understanding. Oh how naïve we are. We waste so much time and energy trying to convince people that we are right when that just may not be the case. We are convinced that all would be well if they would just understand us.

But here is what happens: Each person, certain of their correct vantage point, endeavors to make the other person understand them while making no effort to understand the thinking of that person. It's like having two people in the room each beating their heads against the wall. While each is attempting to convince the other of their perception of the truth of the matter, no understanding of each other is taking place. The more intent we are on convincing them of our correctness, the less chance there is of any understanding taking place.

This brings us to strategy number three for improving our relationships. It is probably not going to sound all that profound, but it is vital to healthy forward progress. Are you ready? Here it is: **Communicate to Understand**

(more than to Be Understood). In other words, *work harder at understanding the other person than you do at making them understand you.* I told you it wouldn't sound all that brilliant. But here is the thing—while two people trying to force each other to understand usually results in no common understanding, two individuals seeking to genuinely understand the other usually results in a clearer grasp of what the other person is saying.

Communicate to Understand

Our relationships are best served when we Communicate to Understand. While that statement may seem obvious, I'm not sure it really is. More often than not, people seem to communicate with the intent of getting the person on the receiving end to change a behavior or to simply get their way.

I often see this goal show up with I Messages. For example, when a wife says, "I feel unimportant when you pay no attention to what I'm saying while you are watching TV. I would like for you to turn the TV down and talk with me."

Now if the husband were to respond with, "I understand that you are feeling discounted when you want to talk with me and I'm unavailable because I am watching sports," his wife is likely to think, "Yes. He got it." However, if the next time she wants to talk while he is watching football, he still doesn't turn the volume down and talk with her, she is likely to be upset. She might say to me, "I used an I Message, but he still kept watching TV. Obviously, I Messages don't work." Well, that is not necessarily true. You see, if your goal is to get your husband to understand your feelings, then this tool was very effective. But if your goal was to change his behavioral response, then you have a point—it doesn't seem to have worked.

Whether we are talking about Reflective Listening or I Messages, our goal is not (or at least shouldn't be) to change behavior. Both of these strategies play a role in strategy three. We are working diligently to understand our mate more than we are working to get them to understand us. Please don't misunderstand me; in the big picture, the more we understand our partner's feelings and thoughts, the better equipped we are to make requested changes. And because we love them and desire to please them, we are more likely to make some changes—once we understand them. But at this point, we are not focusing on changing them, but understanding them.

Can You Help Me Understand?

I want to emphasize one final thought in this chapter. In our efforts to better understand our partner's thoughts, feelings, intentions, priorities, etc., it is easy to go into interrogation mode, asking question after question. While we may be sincerely trying to better comprehend the point our mate is making, we may be honestly struggling to grasp what they are saying. When that happens, it is easy to pepper them with more questions, which may feel to them like an interrogation. That is not our intent. But when we find ourselves in this situation, a phrase/question that I like to use, that cuts straight to the point of what I am trying to accomplish, is this: "Can you help me understand?"

Earlier, in David and Michelle's Thanksgiving scenario, Michelle felt that David wasn't listening, which he wasn't. But even if he had been focused on what she was saying, seeing things from his perspective, he probably still would have struggled to fully comprehend the issue. Had he thrown a barrage of questions at her, she would have likely become frustrated and broken off the conversation all together without any progress. But they might have made headway had David said something like this: "Honey, I hear that you want Thanksgiving to go well. That make perfect sense to me. But I'm a little confused about how you think our parents might be disappointed to the point that they wouldn't want to come back again. Can you help me understand more about that fear?"

Hearing that simple expression of interest and a request for help in learning more about her thoughts and fears, Michelle is likely to feel that he really does care about her feelings. And she will probably be more willing to provide more emotional information that will help him understand. When we feel as though we are being interrogated, we tend to get defensive. But when people ask us to help them, we are much more likely to respond positively. And the chance for understanding increases exponentially!

While you may have begun this journey with only a hammer in your communication tool box, which no doubt was not working well, you should now have three new tools in there at your disposal:

1. Reflective Listening
2. I Messages
3. Communicate to Understand (more than to Be Understood)

Questions to Contemplate

1. Be honest, have you ever thought that you knew best and if your partner would just listen to and understand you then everything would be alright?

2. How might the phrase, "Can you help me understand?" improve your significant other's response?

3. What is likely to be the most difficult thing about Communicate to Understand for you personally?

Chapter Five – "I Know He Is Out to Get Me"

"Assumptions are the termites of relationships." – Henry Winkler

"If we are honest with ourselves, we have to admit that sometimes our assumptions and preconceived notions are wrong, and therefore, our interpretation of events is incorrect. This causes us to overreact, to take things personally, or to judge people unfairly." – Elisabeth Thornton

It was Thanksgiving morning, and Michelle was getting all of the items and ingredients together that she would need for the day. The turkey was defrosted; she had the sweet potatoes ready for the casserole; and she had set the table with their good china. She so badly wanted the day to go perfectly, and she was determined to make it a success. Michelle was glad the parents weren't coming over until later in the afternoon. This would give her plenty of time, with David's help, to have everything ready.

David had been putting in some long hours in previous days, so she was glad he had slept in for a while. She decided to go check on him, as the morning hours were starting to fly by. As she went to see if he was up and showered yet, she heard voices from the bedroom. Opening the door, she discovered that not only was he not up, but he was lying in bed watching the morning football game.

Immediately she thought to herself, "He is being so inconsiderate. He knows how vitally important this day is to me and that I need his help, yet here he is intentionally watching football rather than helping me. He probably wants me to fail! Well, we will see about that." And with those thoughts coursing through her head, she let David have it!

If you are thinking she had an opportunity to use her I Messages or her Reflective Listening tools, you would be absolutely correct. But she didn't. She reached into the tool box and went straight for the hammer. What do you think? Did it work? Of course not. David felt her attack was unjustified. She was accusing him of wanting her to fail, which was the furthest thing from his mind. He was just watching some Thanksgiving football, but here she was talking to him as though he had some diabolical plan to undermine her success. "This is crazy," he thought. "Where is this coming from?"

Practice, Practice, Practice

While I have previously stated that frequent and continuous use of these strategies is critical to making them second nature, this situation with David and Michelle is a perfect example of why that practice is so important. As long as everything is calm and going well, our brains are engaged, and we seem able to use these skills with some effectiveness. But if we find ourselves in a highly emotional or even volatile exchange, our logical thinking shuts down. When that happens, we default to what we know so well— grabbing the hammer and starting to swing. If we were thinking rationally, we would stop, realizing the absurdity of what we are about to do, because we *know* it doesn't work. But thinking rationally is probably the one thing we are not doing. Until we become so proficient with these communication tools that we can basically use them in our sleep, we will find ourselves defaulting to those habits that we know we so badly need to break.

Unfortunately, if you are like many of my client couples, you use one of the strategies three or four times with some measure of success, you have a pretty good week with your mate, and you think, "I've got this." But the reality is, you don't. And then, after a week or two, we are prone to slack off, becoming less diligent in our efforts, and we easily find ourselves right back where we started. As soon as that happens, what do we tend to do? We indignantly state, "That strategy doesn't work," which is partially true. I have been doing this long enough to know the strategies work—but only if you learn, practice, and use them. But if you don't, then they don't.

What Do I Know

The fourth strategy is: **Begin Every Interaction with an Assumption of Positive Intent.** "Well, sure. That makes sense," you may think. And it does make sense, but it is not what we typically do. Take David and Michelle for instance. When Michelle found David calmly watching football in the middle of her Thanksgiving crisis, did she automatically assume, "He must not know my expectations for how much help I need"? No, she squarely landed on: "He doesn't care about me and wants me to fail." She is convinced—thoroughly convinced—she knows his intentions, but the reality is, she doesn't. A cavernous difference exists between knowing what she feels in that moment (which she clearly has a handle on) and what David's intentions are (which she can only guess at best and can easily guess incorrectly).

But here is the funny part (I know because it has happened so many times). If David and Michelle were sitting in my office relating this story, I would be likely to stop them at this point and ask them something that seems to come out of left field. "So, Michelle, tell me what you know about David."

"What do you mean?" she is likely to ask.

"Well, does he love you?"

"Absolutely he does," she replies.

"Does he want good or bad things for you?"

"Good things of course!"

With a sly smirk I may continue, "Is it his desire to throw you in front of a train, or is he pretty protective of you?"

With a chuckle she says, "He always does his best to protect me."

"And these are things that you are sure you know about him?"

"Certainly!"

Then I ask, "Do your thoughts of him being out to sabotage your Thanksgiving and bring you to ruin line up with what you *know* about David?"

Sheepishly she says, "No, I guess they don't."

Again, we get caught up in the emotions of it all. We no longer think straight, and we begin to believe things about our spouse's intentions that don't line up with what we know about the person. When that happens—when what you are feeling about him or her is in conflict with what you know about them—go with what you know. I am going to say that again, because this is extremely important. When what you are feeling about the other person is in direct conflict with who you know them to be—*go with what you know!*

"You want me to fail!"

Allow me to give you an example from my office of how this plays out. A number of years ago, I was working with a couple we will call Josh and Lynda. Josh was a well-established and successful sales associate with a major company. His wife Lynda had worked in the medical field, but had recently left her clinic to pursue her dream of opening her own neighborhood coffee shop. It seems she had toyed with thoughts of being a barista for years, and now was her opportunity.

She had found the perfect location in a newly constructed shopping center that just needed a great coffee shop to be complete. Lynda had some pictures in her mind of what characteristics the inside of her shop would project—cozy, comfortable, inviting, and friendly. She had a good idea of the types of tables, chairs, couches, and wall-hangings that she wanted to create the perfect environment. But she was bumping up against a limited budget.

On the weekends, Josh had been helping Lynda with painting, hanging light fixtures, and whatever else he could do to assist her. After working all of one Saturday at the shop, Josh and Lynda came home exhausted and just sort of collapsed on the couch. But they were able to reflect upon all they had accomplished that day, which felt pretty good. Lynda began to express her anxieties to Josh regarding her budget limitations for furniture. She wanted everything to be just right, but she wanted to be wise with the monies as well. Josh took mental notes.

During the following week, Josh made use of his lunch hours to visit some garage sales and hit some thrift stores after work as well. He found several decent tables and chairs and even some interesting artwork that he thought would work in the coffee shop. Couches were a little more difficult to find in good shape, but he had a friend who had access to some discount furniture that he thought would help Lynda out as well. It was a busy week for Josh, but he was intent on making his wife's dream become a reality.

On Friday night he told Lynda that he had to help a friend move some items into storage (a little fib), while he and a friend actually moved all of the items that Josh had purchased over the course of the week into the coffee shop. Josh wanted to surprise Lynda when they walked in on Saturday morning. He knew she would be relieved, or so he thought.

Saturday morning came, and they were headed to the coffee shop to do so more work. Josh could hardly contain his excitement waiting to see the look on Lynda's face when they opened the front door. As you may have already imagined, when they opened the door, Lynda had a look on her face all right, but not the one that Josh had expected. As she saw all of the furniture, tears began to stream down her face as she cried, "What have you done? Just because you are successful in your career is no reason to keep me from experiencing success with this. I don't know why you want me to fail?" Josh was stunned and speechless.

As they repeated this story in my office the following week, I asked Lynda, "Do you believe that Josh loves you?"

"Well, of course," she replied.

"Does he want good things for you, or does he want to hurt you?" I asked.

Looking a bit bewildered, she said, "He wants good for me!"

"Do you know that for sure?" I continued.

"Absolutely!" she proclaimed.

"Then," I asked, "Does it make sense that he would want you to fail in your new business venture?"

As soon as she realized that what she felt was in conflict with what she knew about him, she moved toward what she knew, and they cleared up the conflict in the time it took to read this narrative. They didn't need to go to separate rooms or punish each other for two days with the silent treatment. They simply needed to examine what they felt in relation to what they knew. This is a foundational principle for this strategy, Begin Every Interaction with an Assumption of Positive Intent.

Every Interaction?

Interactions with our partner are numerous and varied. We could be engaging in discussions about the kid's soccer schedule, whether or not we want to go to our parents' this weekend, what we need at the grocery store, whether we want to have sex tonight, where we should go on vacation, if you like these new shoes, and the list goes on and on. We interact all the time, and all it takes is the smallest feeling of being slighted to derail things. The best strategy for dealing with this is for each of us to begin the interaction with an assumption that the other person has our best interests at heart.

Now you are probably thinking, "Every interaction? I mean, sometimes I think my spouse may have their own interests in mind and couldn't care less about my wants or needs." You are probably correct. "So, if that is the case, how can I begin with an assumption of positive intent?" That's a great question!

Imagine your partner asks you a simple question like, "Where have you been?" If the relationship is going well, that question may come across as one of genuine interest in what you are doing. But if the relationship is more tense and distant, that question can feel parental or accusatory. So, which is it? I have no idea what the intent of the question is, but I do know that how I receive it and respond to it can make a huge difference in the conversation moving forward.

Assuming the person asking me, "Where have you been?" is interested in my experiences or has missed me, makes the question feel nice. It would be easy to respond with, "Oh, I just took the dog out for a quick walk."

"How was it?" they might ask.

"Actually, it was sunny and felt good to get out and move. I ran into Ed while I was out, and it was good to catch up with him."

"That sounds great."

This was an easy, positive interaction. However, what if the person asking me where I have been is questioning me because they think I should have been elsewhere?

"Where have you been?" (You can probably imagine the difference in the tone of voice.)

Now I am feeling differently and might tersely respond, "I was just taking the dog for a walk. Is that OK? Geesh, I didn't know I needed your permission."

"Well, you don't need my permission, but I had some things I wanted you to do, and it would have been nice to know where you were."

"Sorry. I'll be sure to get a hall pass next time!" Needless to say, this didn't go as well.

It is easy to see how, when the interaction begins positively it is easier to maintain the warm feelings. At the same time, when it begins negatively, and the response is negative, the interaction spirals.

But what if no one is around to set up the scenario, as I am doing here? Then there is no way to know the intent of the person asking the question, so I have to start with an assumption of some type.

Let's go back to the first scenario, which was positive, but this time we are going to assume negative intent. What might that look like?

"Where have you been?"

"I just took the dog for a walk. Is that OK with you? It feels as though you monitor my every move, and I'm really getting tired of it."

"What's wrong with you? I was just curious about what you had been doing. I'm sorry I asked you anything." And with that, your spouse leaves the room, and there is silence the rest of the day.

Now let's turn the second scenario around. Again, without me there to set it up, we are in the dark as far as the intent of the person who is asking the question. Here we are going to take what is a more parental, negative question and respond with an assumption of positive intent.

"Where have you been?"

"Oh, it was so nice and sunny out, I took the dog on a short walk. Why do you ask?"

"Well, I had couple of things I needed your help with, and I just wasn't sure where you were. Would you have a few minutes to give me a hand?"

"Sure. Let me just grab a glass of water, and I would be glad to help."

Let's see what we can glean from these four examples. Even though I don't know a person's intent, unless they clearly tell me, if it happens to be positive, and I assume it to be so, the interaction goes well. Yet, even if the intention is positive, if I assume it to be negative, I take the conversation down a dark road.

Similarly, if the person's intent is negative and I assume it will be so, the interaction is dead before it even gets started. But look at what happened when the intent was negative, but I assumed it to be positive: The interaction was salvaged without any hurt feelings.

I think the key to understanding this could be framed this way: Whatever mindset I adopt in beginning an interaction, whether I am the initiator or the recipient, strongly influences how I say what I say and how I hear what I hear. By assuming positive intent, I set up the best possible scenario. And as we saw in the example above, assuming positive intent even in a negative situation can change the tone and the outcome of the conversation. So, even if I am mistaken—assuming they have positive intent when they don't—I have lost nothing and actually may have helped to prevent what could be an ugly conflict.

Think about how this strategy overlays with some of the others. If I assume you are approaching me with the best of intentions, what I see and what I reflect when using Reflective Listening is bound to be wrapped in a more positive light. It changes the very lens through which I see the situation. Using an I Message also helps to steer me away from assuming negative intent. It is always a good idea to ask yourself the question, "What do I know?" You absolutely know what you feel, while you are only making a guess at what your partner's intent is. By saying, "I feel (an emotion), when you do (a behavior)," I am avoiding assuming someone's agenda and actually provide them an opportunity to clarify their intent.

They Work Together

As we have seen, all four of these communication strategies—**Reflective Listening, I Messages, Communicate to Understand (more than to Be Understood), and Begin Every Interaction with an Assumption of Positive Intent**—can individually improve communication. But when we practice and learn to use all four, we find that it is easy to move from one to the other, to use multiple tools at the same time, to improve our understanding and overall communication, and most importantly, to increase the enjoyment of our interactions with the person we most care about.

Questions to Contemplate

1. Do you tend to begin interactions with your spouse from a negative starting point? If so, what do you think most contributes to this tendency?

2. Are there particular topics in which you are most prone to begin with an assumption of negative intent?

3. What do you believe will be most difficult, in the heat of the moment, about leaning on what you know about your partner, as opposed to what you may feel?

SECTION TWO

ADVANCED TOOLS

Chapter Six – "Thank You For What?"

"And the days that I keep my gratitude higher than my expectations, I have really good days." – Ray Wylie Hubbard

"Trade your expectation for appreciation and the world changes instantly." – Tony Robbins

It was a hot summer and a particularly humid afternoon as David came in, sweaty and tired, from mowing the lawn. They had a large yard, and mowing it was one of David's regular chores. He didn't mind doing it, but for some reason today was especially exhausting. As he came in and sat down, he was hoping Michelle would offer to bring him something cold to drink. However, she was busy working on a project and hardly even noticed that David had entered the room. As David sat there, he began to feel annoyed. He thought to himself, "Here I am outside in this extreme heat working my tail off, and when I come in, obviously tired, Michelle doesn't even notice. You would think she would be grateful for my hard work, but I think she has gotten to the point that she just expects it of me." While David didn't say anything, he was feeling unappreciated.

Early that evening, Michelle had cooked one of David's favorite meals — Carne Asada, complete with her homemade guacamole. David was starving and thoroughly enjoyed the meal, nearly licking his plate clean. Following their dinner, they went into the family room to watch some TV. As they sat there, Michelle began to think, "I know David liked the dinner tonight, because he ate everything I put in front of him. But I sometimes wonder if he knows just how much work is required to make all of that happen. You would think he would be grateful, but I think he takes it for granted that I am going to just crank out great meals on a daily basis. I think maybe he takes me for granted." She didn't verbalize any of her thoughts, but she was certainly feeling underappreciated.

Something Just Doesn't Feel Right

As you read the accounts above, you probably realize that neither David nor Michelle were trying to actively discount, dismiss, or ignore the deeds of the other. They had simply grown complacent. They, at some point, had discussed various chores and roles and had come to agreements on who would be responsible for which tasks. David had agreed to be the one who would primarily take care of the lawn and landscaping, while Michelle would be the one who would be responsible for the majority of evening meal preparation. Since they had discussed these areas of responsibility and willingly taken on these respective chores, neither felt as though they had a right to complain. And really, neither wanted to complain, as they preferred their area of responsibility. So what was the issue?

They both had a tough time putting their finger on what was bothering them, which is why neither said anything to the other. Yet, for some reason, they felt unvalued. What had happened is that, without being consciously aware, they both had begun to operate from a place of expectation. In other words, for example, David had agreed to be responsible for the outdoors, so when he did so, he was merely doing what was expected. You don't need to express gratitude or thank someone for doing his or her job—or do you?

Treasuring

During one of the occasions when Jesus was teaching, He said, "Where your treasure is, there your heart will be also" (Matthew 6:21). In other words, where you put your focus is what you will value—what will be most important to you.

In the first section of this book, we learned four strategies that addressed communication issues. As we begin the second half, we will examine issues related to treasuring the other person. These are a little more advanced, because they involve nuances and are not always as obvious as the previous strategies might be. Yet they can have a significant impact on the quality and richness of our relationships. We see this at work as we look at the fifth strategy: Express **Gratitude over Expectation.**

Gratitude vs. Expectation

Have you ever experienced some silly little song lyrics that you will never forget? I still remember words from a song my now grown children learned in Vacation Bible School when they were very young, probably about 30 years ago. The song went like this:
Are you humbly grateful or grumbly hateful?
What's your attitude?
Do you grumble and groan,
Or let it be known
You're grateful for all God's done for you?

Now, hopefully we do not act grumbly hateful toward our spouses, yet we do frequently forget to express humble gratefulness. It doesn't even require much effort. "Honey, thanks for taking the time to fix another fabulous meal tonight." "I know it's not always fun, but I want you to know that I appreciate you going to the grocery store and dealing with the lines." "You are always so consistent about remembering to take the trash out for garbage pick-up day, and I want you to know that I am grateful for that." "You bought a bag of M & M's for me. You always know how much I like those. That was very thoughtful. Thank you!"

You will notice that most of those expressions of thanks are only one or two sentences, which doesn't require a lot of effort. But if that is the case, why do we so often fail to express our gratefulness? That is a terrific question. If we have agreed to take on a particular task or responsibility, we know what is expected. And while we recognize that we don't need to be thanked for doing our job, the truth of the matter is—we still like it. We like when our loved one notices our efforts. We like when they value our efforts. And when they verbally appreciate our efforts, it feels good. As one cellphone company says, "It's not complicated." And it really isn't. But the impact of a "Thank you" can be powerful.

Perhaps you can recall a time at work when your hard work on a project resulted in an acknowledgment in a staff meeting. You probably sat there doing your best not to beam, because the recognition felt great. Or maybe there was a time in school when the teacher called you up to their desk. As you walked up, thinking, "Uh oh, what am I in trouble for?" you were surprised when he or she said, "Hey, nice work on this essay. Thanks for putting in the extra effort." Better still is when your loved one notices you, values what you bring to the table, and tells you so.

I have heard individuals make statements like, "Well, if I am always thanking my spouse for what I would expect them to do, they are liable to get a big head." Really? I have yet to encounter an individual with an inflated ego because their spouse outwardly appreciates them. But I have seen the exact opposite numerous times—when a spouse's efforts are not acknowledged, and as a result, they struggle with low confidence and a diminished self-esteem. I have also heard people say something in their defense like, "If I frequently express appreciation for what they are supposed to do, won't they then expect that all the time?" While I seriously doubt that this would be the result of your efforts at showing gratefulness, even so, what if they did hope for regular signs of appreciation? Is that such a difficult thing?

The nuance of this particular strategy is that while it may not be necessary to avoid conflict, it can play a significant role in strengthening bonds of intimacy. It puts a smile in their heart and draws them in to greater connection. They are more likely to want to be around you and to go the extra mile for you as well. All this happens because of a few words offered in appreciation. When we can receive so much from giving so little, why would we even hesitate to offer words of gratitude?

Changing the Landscape

My dad used to repeat a story that demonstrates the power of gratitude in a relationship. Living in Houston, my dad worked in the tax division of a major oil company. He struggled with the relationship he had with his immediate boss. It seemed as though no matter what my dad did— working overtime, taking on special projects, making sure his work quality was top notch, and so on—his boss was always on his back. Their relationship was tense at best. As you can imagine, he found it difficult to like this individual, and my dad was pretty convinced that his boss, for whatever reason, didn't like him. This certainly made his work situation less than ideal; actually, it was quite stressful. But my dad was not a quitter, and he worked hard to make the best of a difficult situation.

One day, he spotted an article in the company newsletter about his boss and an award that was presented to him at a company luncheon. My dad could have responded in any number of ways. He could have ripped up the article; he could have disparaged his boss behind his back; or he could have simply dismissed it, thinking that his superiors had no idea how difficult this individual was. But what my dad chose to do was very counterintuitive. He sent his boss a card of congratulations on winning the award and thanked him for his leadership. It wasn't a gushy card or some attempt to score points. Dad was simply and respectfully acknowledging his boss' standing in the company and genuinely thanking him for the leadership he provided, even though a lot of his style didn't make too much sense to my dad. My dad did this because he felt it was the right thing, the honoring thing to do, truly not expecting any kind of response.

However, the effects of that simple gesture were truly amazing. The entire demeanor of his boss changed. He began to make it a point to tell my dad, "Good Morning." He would stop by my dad's desk to see how he was doing and whether or not he needed any assistance. He even sent my dad a Christmas card. The temperature of their relationship had completely changed. The old relationship was unrecognizable—all because my dad did something he didn't have to do. My dad's boss was doing his job, which is what he was supposed to do. It didn't require my dad to thank him, especially because he was difficult to deal with. But when my dad did what was unnecessary, the entire relationship was rebuilt with much stronger connections.

Choosing gratitude over expectation can enrich the very fabric of our relationships with our parents, our children, our co-workers, our friends, and yes, even our boss. But most importantly, it can re-energize our connections with our spouse or significant other.

Choosing gratitude over expectation packs so much punch, because that small effort proclaims something truly impactful: "You are important!" "You are a priority!" "You matter to me!" Isn't that how we want our spouse to feel about us? Of course it is, and it is so easily accomplished. It just requires a little awareness mixed with some intentionality. And just like that, you have expressed gratitude.

Learning to use this fifth strategy—Express Gratitude over Expectation—will bless your spouse, improve your marriage, and bring a smile to my face as well. And for that, I thank you!

Questions to Contemplate

1. Do you have more difficulty thanking your spouse for performing a regular household task than you do a co-worker? If so, what do you think contributes to that?

2. What is it that you fear in expressing gratitude to your mate for something that is a part of his or her normal responsibilities?

3. When someone expresses gratitude to you, how does that influence your feelings about them or the relationship?

Chapter Seven – "You Will Never Change!"

"The only way to make sense out of change is to plunge into it, move with it, and join the dance." – Alan Watts

"Getting over a painful experience is much like crossing monkey bars. You have to let go at some point in order to move forward." – C. S. Lewis

Michelle was waiting in the living room as David walked in, having just arrived home from work. David cheerily said "Hi" as he noticed the scowl on Michelle's face. "Where have you been?" she asked with an accusatory tone.

While he wasn't sure what this was about, he clearly knew he was in trouble. "Uh, I've been at work. I just ran a little late getting out of there. Why?"

"Because we are supposed to be at Lynn and Steve's in five minutes for dinner, and you are just now walking in the door!"

"Oh," David responded. "Is that tonight?"

With a look of total frustration, Michelle shot back, "Yes it is tonight! It has been on the calendar for weeks!"

Once again, David had failed to look at the calendar in recent days. This had been an ongoing source of tension between them. They would put things on the calendar hanging in the kitchen, where they both had ready access to it, but it seemed to Michelle as though David never looked at it. They argued about this same issue repeatedly. David would promise to be more diligent, and things would be better for a few days. But then he would default to old patterns of not paying attention to it, and they would be off to the races—having the same argument again.

David wasn't intentionally ignoring the calendar, but he often wasn't being intentional about paying attention to it either. As a result, Michelle felt that what was important to her just didn't matter to him—and perhaps she didn't matter to him. She had begun to feel that she just wasn't a priority.

But here is what is interesting: While this topic had been an ongoing source of frustration for them, after their last conversation about it, David had been on top of it for the last four months—checking the calendar every couple of days . . . until this week.

At this point in their discussion, David was beginning to feel indignant, thinking to himself, "There is just no pleasing her. I have consistently been taking a look at the calendar for months. But this week I dropped the ball, and I am getting pounded, as though I have made no effort or shown no improvement. She hasn't mentioned even once how attentive I have been to this concern for months. But I fail once, and she is all over me about it. She wanted me to make changes, and I have. But I'm not perfect. I'm going to make mistakes. No matter what I do, it's not good enough! What does she expect of me anyway?"

Making Requests for Change

As David noted above, we are not perfect. Therefore, we are faced with the reality that we didn't marry perfect people either. I have yet to find a married individual who doesn't want to change something about his or her mate. It is common. Hopefully, we are not like the woman who stated, "There are all kinds of things I don't like about my fiancé. But it won't be a problem. I will just change him after we are married." Yikes! Not a good plan. This strategy doesn't work, and the marriage usually quickly finds itself in trouble.

What we are talking about here are not wholesale

changes. They are also not changes of personality, as those are more a part of who we are at a basic level. I am speaking about changes of behavior. For example, if dinner is placed on the table and you dive in, consuming half of your food before the rest of the family has even been seated, that is not an unchangeable trait. It is simply a behavior that can be altered.

Or here's another example: Maybe you like to belch crudely when you are in the car with your spouse. While they are offended and even grossed out, you find it rather funny, and so you do it even more. Can you change that behavior? I once heard someone say, "I have to belch, or I will explode. It's just not healthy to restrain myself." The truth is, it is an easily changed behavior—if you believe your partner is worth the effort.

While we could have a discussion as to, "How much change should I make?" or, "Do I need to change everything my spouse wants?" (probably not), those kinds of questions are best saved for another time, as they are outside the scope and purpose of this chapter. The goal here is to better address asking for and accepting change.

Making a request for a husband or wife to change a particular behavior is normal. Demanding change is not loving or effective. However, if we can use our earlier tools, such as I Messages or Communicate to Understand (more than to Be Understood), we are much more likely to make positive headway.

Here is a scenario. I have a tendency (my wife would probably say a strong tendency or maybe even a need) to think and try to get more accomplished in an allotted time frame than is possible. Of course, as that plays out, the result has often been that I'm always running a little behind. This has frequently caused us to run tighter on time, if we have a deadline to be somewhere, than is necessary, and it is certainly avoidable. Having someone, especially your mate, point this out, can result in a defensive response. That may be why my wife's initial approach was to simply tell me that we needed to leave earlier than we really did. But of course, once I figured out what she was doing, I merely adjusted my thinking, knowing that I had more time than she was admitting. Very quickly, we were right back to having to hurry at the last minute. But if my wife were to use an I Message, she might say something like, "I feel embarrassed when we consistently get to a dinner or a concert out of breath, just making it in the nick of time. I would appreciate if you would allow more time in your schedule for getting ready."

Now, while that is certainly a reasonable request, I might still think, "OK, but I don't see what the big deal is" (implying that she is blowing this out of proportion). But at this point, I am going to make the effort to work to *understand her perspective* more than getting my own viewpoint across to her. So I ask, "Can you help me understand why this is so important to you? We always get to where we are going soon enough."

Perhaps she would reply, "As a kid growing up, my dad ran late everywhere we went. If we were going to the movies, we always had to try to find our seats in the dark, having missed the first 10 minutes. If we were going to church, by the time we got there the only seats left were up front, and people starred at us as we walked down the aisle, as the service was already in progress." Suddenly, I would have a new perspective that would serve to increase my desire to make a needed and loving behavioral change.

Accepting the Change

While asking for the change that we want is important,

even that is not the point of this chapter. This next step has a little more subtle nuance. Strategy six is: **Embrace the Change You Have Been Requesting.**

If you find yourself a little puzzled by this strategy, consider this: Have you ever felt like David at the beginning of this chapter, as though no matter what you did, it wasn't good enough? Your spouse requested a change of a particular behavior. You made the change, only to discover that they are no happier than they were before you made the change. As a matter of fact, they may be more unhappy than they were. How can that be?

Recently, the wife of a couple I have been seeing complained about the fact that, for the last ten years, her husband hardly ever demonstrated any affection. He was surprised by this, as all indications to him were that she didn't want to be touched. But he listened attentively and immediately began to make noticeable efforts in the direction she was asking. Yet, following a month of increased affection, she came back into the office angrier than she was before. Why? She had two reasons.

First, as her husband began to do exactly what she was requesting, she realized that he was able to express sincere affection. So why had he wasted the past ten years? He could have been doing this all along! She was furious. While she was correct about the wasted time, he was doing what she asked now. Unfortunately, unless he could invent a time machine, he couldn't go back and fix the last ten years. But he can, and is, dealing with it now. She has a choice. She can either remain upset about what he could have been doing, or she can Embrace the Change She Has Been Requesting.

Second, she may have been complaining about his behavior for so long that it had become a part of her identity. She has felt unloved and, therefore, kept her husband at arm's length. How dare he actually do what she asked? She didn't think he actually would come to the table and make changes. This clearly upset the proverbial apple cart. Her identity as a rejected woman was in danger. And even worse, if her husband has stepped up to the plate to do his part, what behavioral changes might this require of her? Perhaps complaining was easier and even felt a little safer. Now she has another choice. She can maintain a victim mentality (even though she may no longer be a victim) and stay angry at her husband, avoiding any need to change responses on her part, or she can Embrace the Change She Has Been Requesting.

Embracing the Change

As you can see, lots of possibilities exist. Someone may legitimately request their significant other to change a troublesome or annoying behavior. At other times, the request may actually be a ploy to keep the focus off of themselves and their own short-comings. In this case, change isn't honestly what they are looking for. But if the request is genuine, and their partner agrees to and makes the change that is truly desired, healthy connection is within reach. Very simply, if you will accept and Embrace the Change You Have Been Requesting, it will lead to an improvement in your marriage or significant relationship!

Questions to Contemplate

1. Asking for change can get old if there is no follow through. Have you given up? And if so, what kind of resentments are building inside you? What would help you to get past those?

2. What would convince you that your partner's efforts to change are truly happening and are going to stick?

3. If your spouse were to genuinely change the behaviors you have been requesting, what do you fear you would then need to do?

Chapter Eight – "Oh Yea, Well Watch This"

"Let each of you look not only to his own interests, but also to the interests of others." – Philippians 2:4

"The greatest among you shall be your servant." – Matthew 23:11

"This is unbelievable," thought Michelle. Once again David had delicately placed one more item in the wastebasket. It was so full that it was about to spill over onto the floor at any moment. But rather than take the two minutes it would require to empty the trash, David would rather spend three minutes positioning the next piece of garbage in such a manner that it wouldn't topple out. Anything to avoid actually taking care of the trash! It was so silly, but so consistent.

And if she were honest, Michelle had to admit that she did similar things—like leaving the Kleenex box with one tissue in it rather than replacing the box; or leaving the car with practically fumes in the tank rather than stop and fill up with gas. They were both so competitive at not doing things, instead leaving them for the other person to tend to.

Yet at other times, they were more like two ten-year-olds competing over who controlled the television remote or which one of them would choose the restaurant where they would go to eat.

What they didn't seem to notice was how these antics contributed to small annoyances that would build to bigger resentments or how these ongoing competitions would slowly erode positive feelings toward each other. There has to be a better way!

The Suitcase

You may remember the hit television sitcom, "Everybody Loves Raymond." It starred Ray Romano and ran from 1996 to 2005. In one particular episode, Raymond and his wife Debra return from a weekend trip exhausted. They manage to stumble up to bed, leaving their suitcase on the landing of their stairs. After a couple of days, Raymond notices that the suitcase is still there and wonders why Debra hasn't put it away. He figures that since he is at work all day, she should have taken care of it. Then he notices her wearing a sweater she had taken on their trip. That tells him she has unpacked her clothes from the suitcase, but then left it on the landing. What does Raymond do? He gets his clothes out of the suitcase, then puts the suitcase back in the same place on the landing.

The rest of their daily life seems to go along normally, but they are both determined to wait out the other one when it comes to putting the suitcase away. That piece of luggage sits in the same spot for over three weeks, each person determined that he or she will not be the one to put it away. They don't address the topic until their passive-aggressive approach begins to get out of hand.

While this situation made for good comedy on television, immature behavior, like Raymond and Debra's, by real people in a marriage is rarely funny. Instead, it eats away at the very foundation of goodwill and loving feelings. I'm sure you can think of numerous situations that have led to petty competitions—who will finally load the dishwasher; which one will fold the towels that have been sitting on the couch for days; or who will put all of the camping gear away following a trip. And I'm sure you can think of situations you have encountered that I haven't mentioned.

It is mind-numbing the number of childish competitions we engage in with the supposed most important person in our lives. But we don't have to continue this pattern of behavior.

Submission Competition

I like this term, *Submission Competition,* even though I didn't come up with it. Pastor Andy Stanley did. Now I know that, in the twenty-first century, many struggle with the idea of submission. For some reason, we associate this word with being inferior, not having our own identity, or allowing someone else to control us. But that is not what is meant here at all. Rather, it is an intentional choice that we make to elevate someone else to a place of priority. I am not saying they are superior or more important than you. What I am emphasizing is that it can be loving to "do for" the other.

My wife isn't necessarily a fan of the word *serve* when I use it, but because I love her, I take pleasure in serving her. By this I don't mean that I run around like a puppy dog catering to her every whim. Neither do I mean that if I don't meet her every desire I will be in trouble, so I need to keep her happy in order to "keep the peace."

An example of this can be something as simple as bringing my wife coffee every morning. Does she expect this? No. Does she enjoy it? Yes. Does it communicate love? Absolutely. And I enjoy doing it. Following this line of thinking comes Strategy seven: **Compete to Out-Serve Each Other.**

Competition with your husband or wife is not necessarily negative; it just depends on what you are competing for. When competition is about getting out of doing something or making more work for our mate, it doesn't serve to build stronger bonds. In fact, it does the exact opposite. But what happens when we compete to out-serve the other? Believe me when I tell you that in all of my years of counseling, I have never had a husband or wife come into my office and complain that their spouse is serving or loving them too much.

So, what does this look like in practicality? I will give you two examples from my own marriage. Now, please don't think I am holding myself up as though I have learned to always execute this effectively, because I haven't. It's just that I understand the concept and sometimes actually get it right.

While a common complaint I hear from couples has to do with who is going to load or unload the dishwasher, you won't hear that complaint in our household—at least not in its usual form. When we finish a meal, my wife will usually say, "I'll take care of the dishes. You go do whatever you need to do." However, if she cooked, which she does most of the time, because she is a much better cook than I am, I want her to relax, and I am happy to take care of the dishes. So, sometimes this can turn into a competition as to who gets to "do for" the other by doing the dishes.

Similarly, when the dishwasher needs to be unloaded, I have been known to try to get to the dishwasher first, sometimes starting to unload the dishes while they are still almost too hot to handle. My wife, with appreciation on her face will say, "You are ridiculous." And I am pleased.

My second silly example has to do with my wife's car. Occasionally, when running some errands, we will go in my wife's vehicle. Sometimes, in the course of the outing, she may need to stop for gas. When that happens, invariably she will state that she will put the gas in the car.

To that I respond, "No, I will."

Her next response is usually something along the lines of, "You don't have to do that. I can put gas in my car."

Now, somewhat tongue-in-cheek, I will say, "No, you can't do that."

I know the rise I will get out of her, as she smiles and says, "Oh, are you saying I'm not capable of putting gas in the car? What do you think I do when you're not here?"

"But, I am here. And as long as I'm here, I will fill the tank," I reply. "Honey, I know that you are more than capable and that you do it all the time when I am not around. But I am your husband, and as long as I am here, I will take care of it."

"Well, but you don't need to feel as though you have to do it," she continues.

"I don't feel obligated; I want to do it for you."

Is filling the car with gas that big of a deal? Of course not, but she feels honored, and I get to take advantage of the opportunity to demonstrate love—especially if it's snowing outside.

There are many examples of mundane or even unpleasant tasks that we could throw out for discussion. Let's face it, there is nothing particularly fun or attractive about doing dishes, folding laundry, taking out the trash, vacuuming the house, and so on. But each of these provide an opportunity for us to demonstrate love to our spouse and, in doing so, to communicate: "You are worthy."

I know that someone is likely to say, "But if I try to be the first to do things of this nature, he or she will let me do everything while they sit on the couch and do nothing. That's not fair. I will be totally taken advantage of!" While this is certainly a possibility, I am hoping that perhaps your spouse is also reading this book or perhaps you are even reading it together.

As with any of these strategies, there are no guarantees

that your mate will necessarily engage as quickly or at the same level of diligence as you do. But here is what I can tell you—if you will implement this idea of out-serving your husband or wife, it is likely that you will begin to change the current dynamics of your relationship. And that offers the hope of forward relational progress.

Bottom Line

If you are like most of us, you probably have years of experience in competing with your spouse to avoid certain tasks or responsibilities. I imagine this has led to more than one argument (perhaps several), and they have likely been repeated more times than you care to admit. Aren't you weary of this battling?

As I mentioned earlier, I see couples on a daily basis engaged in needless negative competitions that have ripped the joy right out of their marriage. Their foundation has become fragile, and they no longer feel cared for by the other.

Conversely, when I see a couple Compete to Out-Serve Each Other, I have yet to hear a complaint. The individuals do not feel slighted or taken advantage of. Instead, what I witness is increased bonding and feelings of safety, validation, love, and importance. Isn't that what you want your spouse to feel? Isn't that what you want to experience as well?

You know that your old, tired ways of competing have only led to damage in your relationship. Maybe it's time to try competition from an entirely new vantage point. Who knows, you just might improve your marriage.

Questions to Contemplate

1. What is the number one issue over which you and your spouse typically get locked into an "I'm never giving in" battle or competition?

2. How do you feel when you win those competitions? How do you feel when you lose?

3. What can you do to begin to compete in out-serving your mate? How difficult will that be for you?

Chapter Nine – "Hmm, I Had Forgotten about That"

"Too often we make the mistake of remembering what we should forget—our hurts, failures and disappointments—and we forget what we should remember—our victories, accomplishments and the times we have made it through." – Joel Osteen

"It takes one thought, one second, one moment or positive memory to act as a catalyst for the light to gradually seep in again." – Fearne Cotton

David had looked forward to having lunch with his friend Bryan for a couple of days. But here he was, moving his food around on his plate, dejected and hardly paying attention to whatever it was that Bryan was talking about.

Finally, Bryan made one of those comments that you might make when you can see that the other person's mind is somewhere else—"And then I jumped out of the plane without a parachute and was flattened when I hit the ground."

David responded, "That's nice."

At that point, Bryan said, "David, what's going on? You've hardly touched your food, and you are totally disengaged from this conversation."

Looking up, startled by Bryan's comment, David replied, "I'm sorry. I know I am probably not very good company today. I just can't shake an argument that Michelle and I had this morning. I'm beginning to wonder why Michelle even married me."

"What do you mean?" asked Bryan."

"Well, I am convinced she doesn't love me. I mean, I don't know that she even thinks about me if I'm not standing right in front of her. Her mind is always somewhere else."

"Wow," exclaimed Bryan. "That doesn't sound like the Michelle I've heard you talk about before."

Caught off guard, David asked, "What do you mean?"

"I just know that in the past you have described her quite a bit differently. For example, a month ago you said she had purchased a new shirt for you out of the clear blue for no particular reason. Then a couple weeks ago, you mentioned that she had been out at the bookstore café and brought a couple cookies home for you. It sure sounds to me like she was thinking about you."

Sitting there with a furrowed brow, contemplating what he just heard, David finally spoke. "You know what? I must admit I had forgotten about those incidents. And actually, there are a lot more than that. Michelle frequently tells me how proud she is of my accomplishments at work, and she is always saying that she loves me. I guess it is just easy after an argument to think the worst and that things are awful. But really, if I would just remember, they aren't."

Revisionist History

Inadvertently, David had become caught up in the emotions of the moment, extrapolating conclusions that simply were not accurate. He was rewriting the history of their relationship in a way that placed a dark and seemingly insurmountable cloud over it. It is easy to do.

This brings us to strategy eight: **Remember Accurately.**

I want to share here an excerpt from my book, *Unstuck: Escaping the Rut of a Lifeless Marriage*, regarding this strategy.

> With regularity I listen as couples tell me how they have never trusted their spouse, never been happy with them, and

aren't even certain that they every really loved them. Yet, if I am able to get an account of events of their life, whether it is from themselves, friends, or family, I will typically get a more complete picture. Couples who have been wounded by each other over time frequently engage in what I call "revisionist history." One such couple sat in my office this past month doing exactly that.

With their marriage crashing against the rocks, David and Trina called for an appointment. Their marriage had almost gone sideways a few years earlier, but David had realized some mistakes he had made and proclaimed a renewed love and dedication to his wife. Best of all, he backed it up with action. But here they were two years later with David having been caught in an extra-marital affair. They were in serious trouble. While I would like to say that David really figured it out this time, acknowledged his grave error, and deeply repented to his wife—that is not what happened. Instead, he said that this was all her fault. He began by narrating how she had flirted with a man at a business party about 10 years ago. While a big argument had ensued at the time, he had recognized that it was an unintentional wound on her part and they worked through it.

Yet now, 10 years later, that event had taken on a significance previously unseen.

What was actually happening was "revisionist history." Whether it was because he had forgotten how well they had mended things and how much love he had felt for his wife then or it was because revising history served his purposes to justify behavior now—the results were the same. He was working to create a new version of reality.

It is **especially** at the low times of a marriage that an accurate recollection is important. It is highly unlikely that we would marry someone because we never liked them in the first place, we couldn't trust them, and we thought they were ugly. If that were true—then we needed some intense therapy back then. Recalling the positives that led to our marriage in the first place is needed during the difficult times. When things are bad—we have a tendency to rewrite history and convince ourselves that things have never been good so we had better get out of this awful marriage. I hear individuals say, "I don't love him anymore. As a matter of fact, I'm not sure I ever did." This is revisionist history on display.

Remembering the positives in our relationship is essential to our marital health and our commitment to one another. If reengagement is to have a chance, we have to remember the real story.

Forgetting Seems to be Our Default Mode

Our tendency to forget important commitments, experiences, and feelings is not uncommon. This has been a problem for humankind since the beginning of time. On numerous occasions, as recorded in scripture, God blessed and took care of His people, the nation of Israel, only to have them quickly forget about all He had done for them. One example of this is found in Exodus 32.

After nearly 400 years in slavery in Egypt, God called Moses to go to the Pharaoh (much like a King) and proclaim those famous words, "Let my people go." The short version of the story is that after God used ten plagues to convince Pharaoh that this would be a smart move for him to make, he did. Israel left with everything they owned as well as gold and silver given to them by many of the Egyptians. The people were finally free because of God's favor and His power.

It wasn't long before Pharaoh had a change of heart and gathered his army to capture Israel and bring them back to Egypt. With Pharaoh in hot pursuit, Israel's march led them right to the shore of the Red Sea. Now what? Well, as I'm sure you know, God parted the sea for the people and led them safely across. While we may have heard the narrative repeated hundreds of times, I don't think we stop and think about the power it would take to split a sea and create a safe, dry path for these people. But God, the only One capable of performing this feat, did that very thing for the people He cherished.

So, God had led them out of slavery with riches; had miraculously landed them on the other side of the Red Sea; and had now brought them to wait at the base of Mt. Sinai while Moses received the Ten Commandments from God. God was in no hurry, and Moses remained with God for

40 days. No big deal—or at least it shouldn't have been. God had demonstrated that He would take care of His people.

But it became a big deal. As the people grew impatient, they seemed to have forgotten all the things God had so recently done to rescue them. So, what did they do? They compelled Aaron, Moses' brother, to take the gold and silver the people had, melt it down, and create a golden calf. This would be their god who would lead them back to Egypt. Really? You can't make this stuff up. How very quickly they forgot.

We might think, "Oh, what a forgetful people they were." But I would submit, "What a forgetful people we are." One day we are standing with our spouse, before a gathering, and proclaiming our undying love for each other, and the next we seem to have forgotten all of that. It is so easy in difficult situations to forget the good times. This is why this eighth strategy, Remember Accurately, is so critical.

Ideas to Help with Accurate Recollection

Couples can use any number of creative ideas to remember the things that have actually represented bright and healthy times in their relationship. I would like to suggest a few that I have seen work effectively for many couples.

1) Make use of photos and videos. I love pictures— probably because I am a visual person.

For decades I would take pictures, print them out, and put them in photo albums. I have lots of those albums. More recently I have begun to put both pictures and videos into a DVD or Flash-drive format. I video birthdays, Christmases, or just the grandkids and their hilarious antics. These don't just sit somewhere in "the cloud," wherever that is. They are where I can watch and re-watch them over the years. You see, they anchor the veracity of real events.

2) Embrace traditions. These are things you put into place to be repeated on a regular

basis. This might include watching your wedding video every anniversary or making an annual trek to the restaurant or location where you went on your first date and talking about what attracted you to each other. There are so many possibilities.

3) Retell the stories of how you met and fell in love— anything about the highlights or

successful struggles of your marriage—to friends, couples, kids, grandkids, parents, or anyone who will listen. It is so easy to talk about our mate's negative behaviors and overlook the positives. Yet, retelling the positive stories fosters connection and feelings of love.

4) Be mindful. As author Brené Brown says, being mindful is a fancy way of saying

"Pay attention." Make it a point to think about your spouse. By that I mean, pay attention to various parts of your marriage that will assist your heart in following your head's lead. For example, even if you need to put it on a calendar, pay attention to significant dates—birthdays, anniversaries, and so on. Make it a point during the course of your work day to take 30 seconds and text your spouse to simply say, "I'm thinking of you," "I love you," or "I hope your day is going well." Paying attention strengthens our bonds of connection.

With the nation of Israel, God instituted a number of festivals, holidays, and feasts because He knew these events would help people remember the ways He had loved and protected them. Similarly, putting concrete anchors in place to help us Remember Accurately can make the difference between feelings of regret and emotions of gratitude and hopefulness. This strategy can absolutely play a role in improving your relationship!

Questions to Contemplate

1. What is it, do you believe, that so frequently leads us to rewrite history or to modify our story as couples?

2. What does re-writing history gain for you?

3. What things can you personally put in place to ensure that you Remember Accurately?

Chapter Ten – Firing on All Cylinders . . . Most of the Time

"We, in fact, determine how skilled we become in the sense that if we choose not to practice, we recognize that we will not move beyond the point at which we stopped." – Byron Pulsifer

"Practice makes progress." – Anonymous

"The more you sweat in practice, the less you bleed in battle." – Norman Schwarzkopf

You may recall from the beginning of this book just how carefully David and Michelle had approached their relationship. They listened to wise counsel, took things slowly, and avoided so many of the mistakes they had seen their friends make. Each felt, and truly believed, they were marrying their perfect mate. I had said, they "were destined for a beautiful and fulfilling life together. And they were . . . but perhaps with a few bumps along the way."

You may be thinking, "Well since that first encounter with them, that's all we have seen . . . bumps." And you are correct, but that has been by design. They have experienced many wonderful times. However, those examples would not have helped us to best see and understand the application of the eight strategies for improving our own relationships. So, without being Pollyannaish, let's peek in on them when they utilize these skills.

The Reunion

This was destined to be a weekend to remember. The 10th of June would mark 30 years that David and Michelle had been married. But not only were they going to celebrate that milestone, it just so happened that their anniversary was coinciding with their planned family reunion. Their son Joshua and his wife, their daughter Julie, David's parents, and Michelle's mother would all be there. Michelle's dad had passed the previous year and would be greatly missed.

It was the day before the reunion, and David's parents would be arriving at the airport that afternoon. As David told Michelle that he was leaving to pick up his parents, she said, "So you are going to the airport and then you are coming home. Right?"

"No," he replied. "Remember, I told you yesterday that I have to stop at Josh's house and pick up a couple of extra chairs?"

"Oh, that's right. I had forgotten that you told me that. I'm glad I checked-in." **[Reflective Listening]**

By the time David arrived home with his parents, three hours had passed, and Michelle had been a little concerned that this had taken David so long. What she discovered was that his parents had not eaten since before they boarded the plane that morning and were starved. So, they made a stop to grab a bite before coming home.

Later that evening, when they were alone, Michelle said to David, "While I certainly understand that your mom and dad needed something to eat today, I need to tell you that I felt unimportant when you didn't call to let me know that you were making that extra stop. I would appreciate it if in future situations you would just give me a quick heads-up." **[I Message]**

Thoughtfully, David responded, "You know what? You are right. I should have given you a call. While it's no excuse, I just got caught up visiting with my parents and spaced letting you know. I'm sorry, and I will attempt to be better aware in the future."

"Thanks David. I appreciate that."

The next day was the big day! Michelle was working feverishly to get all of the food prepared, setting the table, and making sure everyone had what they needed. She was hoping for some help from David, but he was nowhere to be found. Then, looking out the window, she spotted David and Josh out in the driveway shooting hoops. While she was mildly irritated, she figured there must be a reason, because he knew how much work she had to do.

Later, when David had come back into the house, she started to say, "What are you doing playing basketball when you know how much there is still to do to get ready for this evening?" But she caught herself, and instead asked, "I know you are aware of how much preparation we still have to do. Can you help me understand why you were out playing while I'm in here working?"

"Sure," he replied. "Josh is having some unusual challenges at work that he really wanted to talk with me about. And you know how much more open he is when he has a basketball in his hands. It was worthwhile time. I knew that you needed help. I just felt that talking with him took precedence in the moment. But I am here now, and I am at your disposal," he said with a smile.

She responded, "I do understand, and I appreciate the explanation, but I will take your help now." **[Communicate to Understand (more than to Be Understood)]**

After helping Michelle, David went into the garage where his dad was hanging out. Almost immediately, his dad questioned him, "How come you've never put up the ping-pong table your mom and I gave you?" Sensing an accusatory tone in his dad's voice, he almost responded defensively, but then stopped himself, knowing that wouldn't go well. He knew that from past experiences.

Instead he said, "You know dad, Michelle and I have been talking about that. We know that you just want us to enjoy playing, and I was hoping to get it set-up this weekend while you and Josh are both here. I need some muscle to get it downstairs."

"That sounds great son. I will be happy to help." **[Begin Every Interaction with an Assumption of Positive Intent]**

As they finished talking, Michelle popped her head out the door and asked David when he planned to get the coals started in the grill. David told her he had actually done that before he came out to the garage. Michelle simply said, "Thanks. You are so good about being on top of that kind of stuff." **[Express Gratitude over Expectation]**

As dinner time neared, Michelle's phone rang. It was Julie. She was calling to say she was running late. "Again?" thought Michelle. She was about to go into parent lecture mode, as Julie had a track record of poor planning and running late, but she paused and took a deep breath. She knew that would not be productive. This had been a long-standing problem for Julie. People made jokes about it as well as often complained in frustration. But about three months earlier, she and Julie had had a heart-to-heart discussion about the issue. Michelle gained some understanding as to the reasons Julie consistently ran late, and Julie began to grasp the frustration that others felt with this habit. In that conversation, Julie had made a commitment to change this pattern of behavior. And amazingly, she hadn't been late anywhere in those months.

Michelle had suggested the benefits of changing this behavior to Julie, and Julie had responded well. The last thing Julie needed was somebody asking something like,

"Why are you always late?" Because truth be told, Julie wasn't always late. This was the first time in three months. Instead, Michelle attempted to acknowledge that progress by listening this time with an understanding ear. **[Embrace the Change You Have Been Requesting]**

The family reunion, along with the anniversary celebration, went fabulously. The weekend exceeded expectations. The kids had returned to their homes, along with Michelle's mom, and David had taken his parents back to the airport. Now it was just Michelle and David at home again, both rather exhausted. They needed to clean-up, take the extra leaves out of the table, get the towels and sheets in the laundry—and the list went on. They both said they would do it, but they were too tired (it was a good tired) to move, barely making it into bed. They fell asleep quickly, but David woke up a couple hours later. Since he was awake, he decided to quietly sneak into the other room and start a load of laundry and get the clean dishes put away. He wanted his wife to rest as well as be surprised in the morning. However, as he headed for the kitchen, he found Michelle already doing what he had in mind. They took one look at each other and broke out laughing. Obviously they had both had the same thoughts. **[Compete to Out-Serve Each Other]**

Sitting on the couch the following weekend, they pulled out their phones and together looked at all of the pictures and video footage they had taken during their reunion/anniversary weekend. This led to conversations on how good it was to see everyone and how fortunate they each felt to have arrived at this 30-year mark, still so much in love and more committed than ever to each other. It was a satisfying look back and would be for years to come. **[Remember Accurately]**

Using These Strategies

While the narrative above may seem a little too perfect, it is merely a picture of the other side of the previous chapter's stories with major mistakes. But it does illustrate how much differently things can go and the kind of improvements that can truly be made by putting into practice these eight specific strategies.

Wouldn't you like to see these kinds of improvements in your own marriage or relationship? You can! The benefits of implementing these steps include tearing down walls between you and your spouse and learning again to trust, love, enjoy, thrill at the sight of, and cherish each other again. It is absolutely within your reach if . . .

"Oh, there is that 'if' again." Yes there is. If you will learn, put into practice, fail at, practice some more, not give up, and persevere until these eight strategies become second nature.

I want to share with one of my blog posts from a few years ago that clearly drives home this concept of practicing until patterns of relating change to the point that these new strategies become your natural reactions.

On July 6, 2013, Asiana Airlines Flight 214 from South Korea crashed short of the runway at the San Francisco Airport. The plane struck the ground with the tail hitting a seawall. Three flight attendants were ejected. One of the remaining flight attendants, Lee Yoon-Hye, helped hundreds of passengers get safely out of the plane and onto the runway.

When an emergency slide deployed improperly, Lee handed a knife to the co-pilot who punctured the slide. When she saw flames erupt, she tossed a fire extinguisher to a colleague. It was later discovered that she did all of this with a broken tailbone.

You may be thinking, "OK, a heroic story, but how does that relate to me?" Here is the point: Lee was able to perform at this level in a crisis, in part, because their flight training is intense. They practice and practice evacuating a plane until they are able to empty a jumbo jet filled with passengers in 90 seconds. Then when a real crisis happens, as it did on that flight, they just follow their training.

Wouldn't it be nice if we were able to similarly respond to crises in our significant relationships with that kind of deftness? Instead, many couples hit a stressful situation and implode or have some kind of meltdown. Rather than work as a team, as Lee and her colleagues did, it's easy for us to turn on each other.

What if we practiced? What if when times are good we had honest conversations about crises that we are likely to face? What if we spent time reading books with our partner about ways to improve our relationship? What if we went to a weekend marriage retreat with our spouse? What if (intimacy at its best) we prayed with our spouse?

It would be wonderful to be trained to respond to a marital or family crisis successfully in 90 seconds. I encourage you to explore with your mate today how the two of you can better prepare for life's unexpected curve balls.

And I would add to these thoughts—one of the best ways to prepare for life's curve balls is to diligently become a student of these eight strategies, practicing them until you master them. Will things be perfect? I highly doubt it. But will it be better? If you will take to heart and put into practice what you have read, I guarantee that you will significantly improve your relationship!

Questions to Contemplate

1. Which of these strategies have you already been doing pretty well with? You might check with your husband or wife to verify accuracy on this.

2. Which of these eight strategies do you fear will be the most difficult for you to effectively put in place?

3. Since you know that using these new skills will improve your marriage/relationship, what steps will you take to help these responses become second nature for you?

Quick Strategy Reference Guide

1. Make sure you are on the same page by using Reflective Listening
2. Practice emotional honesty by using I Messages.
3. Communicate to Understand (more than to Be Understood).
4. Begin Every Interaction with an Assumption of Positive Intent.
5. Express Gratitude over Expectation.
6. Embrace the Change You Have Been Requesting.
7. Compete to Out-Serve Each Other.
8. Remember Accurately.

ABOUT THE AUTHOR

BARRY D, HAM, Ph.D. is a Licensed Marriage and Family Therapist, college professor, author, and speaker and has been working with individuals and couples in Colorado Springs for nearly 25 years, and professionally for over 35 years. His educational background includes a Master's degree in psychology from Abilene Christian University, a Master's degree in Marriage, Family, and Child counseling from California State University, and a Doctorate in Clinical Psychology from Southern California University.

Barry's passion is to work with individuals, couples and families struggling through the transitions of life. He believes that change is absolutely possible and that people do not have to settle for and endure poor relationships – they can be repaired, renewed, and restored. Life was meant to be lived to the fullest with vibrant, supportive, and loving relationships as an essential part of it. Couples can experience full, healthy, and complete lives physically, mentally, emotionally, and spiritually, moving beyond the past to live fully in the present.

Barry lives in the Colorado Springs area with his wife and their Goldendoodle, Jolee. He and his wife have grown children whose families live in Colorado and Florida, and they have four grandkids.

CONTACT INFORMATION

Dr. Ham is available to speak at your church or gathering and also available for weekend seminars.

For booking and additional information, he can be contacted at:

Dr. Barry D. Ham

c/o Integrative Family/Individual Therapy

P.O. Box 63241

Colorado Springs, CO 80962

drbdham@msn.com

www.livingonpurpose.net

Made in the USA
Monee, IL
24 September 2021